KIDS ON EARTH

Wildlife Adventures – Explore The World
Tortoise - Ecuador

Sensei Paul David

COPYRIGHT PAGE

Kids On Earth: Wildlife Adventures - Explore The World

Tortoise - Ecuador

by Sensei Paul David,

Copyright © 2023.

All rights reserved.

978-1-77848-183-3 KoE_WildLife_Amazon_PaperbackBook_ecuador_tortoise

978-1-77848-182-6 KoE_WildLife_Amazon_eBook_ecuador_tortoise

978-1-77848-421-6 KoE_Wildlife_Ingram_Paperbackbook_Tortoise

This book is not authorized for free distribution copying.

www.senseipublishing.com

@senseipublishing
#senseipublishing

Synopsis

This fun and educational book explores the fascinating world of the Ecuadorian tortoise. Through exciting facts and colorful illustrations, children will learn all about these amazing animals and the incredible habitats they live in. From their diet and behavior to the unique adaptations they have evolved over millions of years, this book will provide an in-depth look at the fascinating lives of these majestic creatures. From the rainforests of the Amazon to the highlands of the Andes, the Ecuadorian tortoise has learned to survive in many different climates. With fun facts and colorful illustrations, this book is sure to be a hit with kids of all ages!

Get Our FREE Books Now!

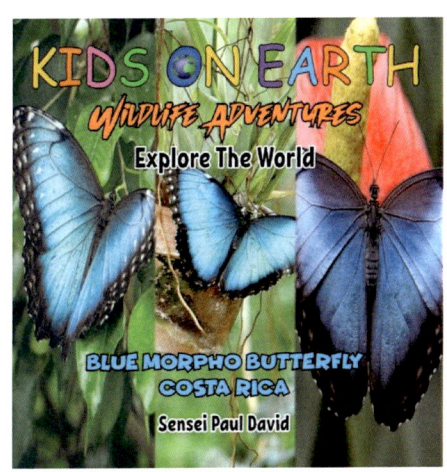

kidsonearth.life

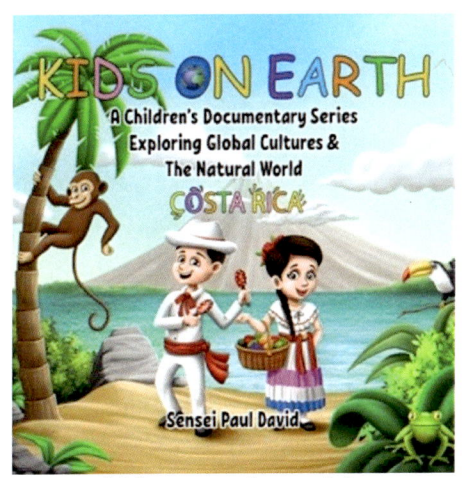

kidsonearth.world

Click Below for Another Book In Each Series

senseipublishing.com/KoE_SERIES

senseipublishing.com/KoE_Wildlife_SERIES

KoE En Español

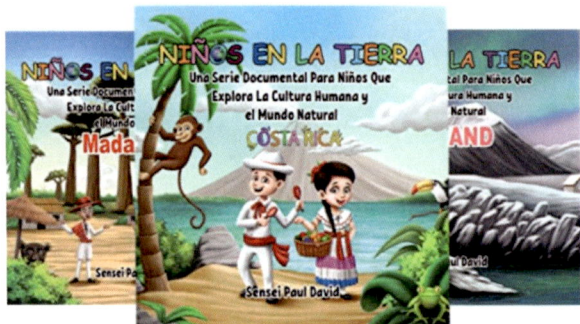

senseipublishing.com/KoE_SERIES_SPANISH

www.senseipublishing.com

Join Our Publishing Journey!

If you would like to receive FUTURE FREE BOOKS and get to know us better, please click www.senseipublishing.com and join our newsletter by entering your email address in the pop-up box.

Follow Our Blog: senseipauldavid.ca

Follow/Like/Subscribe: Facebook, Instagram, YouTube: @senseipublishing

Scan the QR Code with your phone or tablet to follow us on social media:

Like / Subscribe / Follow

Introduction

Welcome to the wonderful world of the Ecuadorian tortoise! These amazing creatures have been around since the time of the dinosaurs and are still thriving today. This fun and educational book will help children learn all about these incredible animals and the incredible habitats they live in. From their diet and behavior to the unique adaptations they have evolved over millions of years, this book will provide an in-depth look at the fascinating lives of these majestic creatures. From the rainforests of the Amazon to the highlands of the Andes, the Ecuadorian tortoise has learned to survive in many different climates. With exciting facts and colorful illustrations, this book is sure to be a hit with kids of all ages!

Ecuadorian tortoises are one of the oldest species of tortoises in the world, dating back to the age of dinosaurs.

They can live up to 150 years or more in the wild.

These tortoises are found in the tropical rainforests, grasslands, and highlands of Ecuador.

They are omnivores and feed on a variety of plants and insects.

These tortoises have a high level of camouflage, which helps them blend in with their environment.

They are solitary animals, preferring to live alone or in small groups.

The Ecuadorian tortoise is an endangered species due to habitat loss and poaching.

They are one of the few species of tortoises that live in both water and on land.

The Ecuadorian tortoise has an extremely long neck and can stretch it up to two feet.

They can also retract their head and neck into their shells when threatened.

These tortoises are great climbers and can even climb trees if necessary.

They are usually active during the day and sleep at night.

The Ecuadorian tortoise is a slow-moving animal and can travel up to three miles per hour.

They use their long claws to dig burrows and to climb trees.

They are not territorial and are often seen sharing their burrows with other animals.

The Ecuadorian tortoise can live in a variety of habitats, from the lowlands to the highlands of the Andes.

They are mostly herbivorous, but will sometimes eat small animals such as insects and worms.

These tortoises can live in temperatures ranging from 50 to 95 degrees Fahrenheit.

The Ecuadorian tortoise is believed to be a symbol of longevity and wisdom in some cultures.

The females lay between two to five eggs in a clutch.

The hatchlings are independent from the moment they emerge from their eggs.

The Ecuadorian tortoise is known to have a long lifespan in captivity, up to 200 years.

They communicate with each other through vocalizations.

They have a very poor sense of smell, but their vision is very good.

These tortoises can travel up to 20 miles in a single day.

The Ecuadorian tortoise is a popular pet and can be found in many pet stores.

They are also used in traditional medicine in some cultures.

The Ecuadorian tortoise can live in both salt and freshwater habitats.

They are active all year round and hibernate in the winter months.

The Ecuadorian tortoise is an important part of the ecosystem, helping to disperse seeds and disperse nutrients in the soil.

Conclusion

The Ecuadorian tortoise is an amazing and unique creature that has been around for millions of years. They are a part of the rich biodiversity of Ecuador and are an important part of the ecosystem. From their diet and behavior to their unique adaptations, this book has provided an in-depth look at the fascinating lives of these majestic creatures. With fun facts and colorful illustrations, this book is sure to be a hit with kids of all ages.

Thank you for reading this book!

If you found this book helpful, I would be grateful if you would **post an honest review on Amazon** so this book can reach other supportive readers like you!

All you need to do is digitally flip to the back and leave your review. Or visit amazon.com/author/senseipauldavid click the correct book cover and click on the blue link next to the yellow stars that say, "customer reviews."

As always...

It's a great day to be alive!

Share Our FREE eBooks Now!

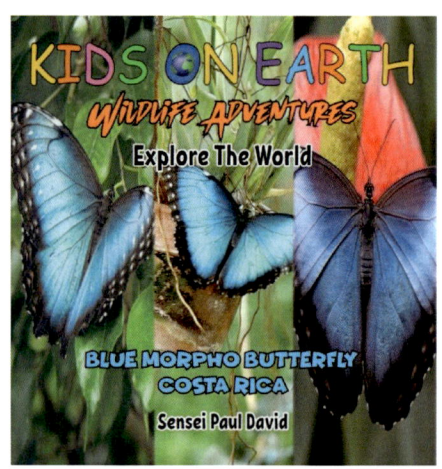

kidsonearth.life

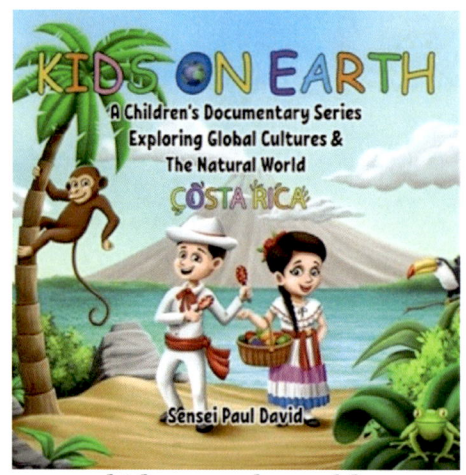

kidsonearth.world

Click Below for Another Book In Each Series

senseipublishing.com/KoE_SERIES

senseipublishing.com/KoE_Wildlife_SERIES

KoE En Español

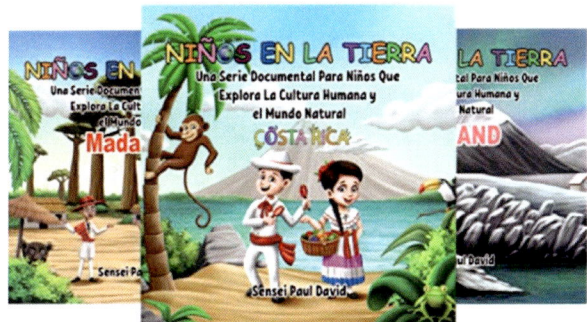

senseipublishing.com/KoE_SERIES_SPANISH

www.senseipublishing.com

www.senseipublishing.com

@senseipublishing
#senseipublishing

Check out our **recommendations** for other books for adults & kids plus other great resources by visiting
www.senseipublishing.com/resources/

Join Our Publishing Journey!

If you would like to receive FREE BOOKS and special offers, please visit www.senseipublishing.com and join our newsletter by entering your email address in the pop-up box

Follow Our Engaging Blog NOW!
senseipauldavid.ca

Get Our FREE Books Today!

Click & Share the Links Below

FREE Kids Books

lifeofbailey.senseipublishing.com
kidsonearth.senseipublishing.com

FREE Self-Development Book

senseiselfdevelopment.senseipublishing.com

FREE BONUS!!!
Experience Over 25 FREE Engaging Guided Meditations!

Prized Skills & Practices for Adults & Kids. Help Restore Deep Sleep, Lower Stress, Improve Posture, Navigate Uncertainty & More.

Download the Free Insight Timer App and click the link below:
http://insig.ht/sensei_paul

About Sensei Publishing

Sensei Publishing commits itself to helping people of all ages transform into better versions of themselves by providing high-quality and research-based self-development books with an emphasis on mental health and guided meditations. Sensei Publishing offers well-written e-books, audiobooks, paperbacks, and online courses that simplify complicated but practical topics in line with its mission to inspire people toward positive transformation.

It's a great day to be alive!

About the Author

I create simple & transformative eBooks & Guided Meditations for Adults & Children proven to help navigate uncertainty, solve niche problems & bring families closer together.

I'm a former finance project manager, private pilot, jiu-jitsu instructor, musician & former University of Toronto Fitness Trainer. I prefer a science-based approach to focus on these & other areas in my life to stay humble & hungry to evolve. I hope you enjoy my work and I'd love to hear your feedback.

- It's a great day to be alive!
Sensei Paul David

Scan & Follow/Like/Subscribe: Facebook, Instagram, YouTube: @senseipublishing

Scan using your phone/iPad camera for Social Media
Visit us at www.senseipublishing.com and sign up for our newsletter to learn more about our exciting books and to experience our FREE Guided Meditations for Kids & Adults.

www.ingramcontent.com/pod-product-compliance
Lightning Source LLC
Chambersburg PA
CBRC090902080526
44587CB00008B/174